HOW TO DO CHI SAO

WING CHUN STICKY HANDS

Sam Fury

Illustrations by Alexander Sheshikov

Contents

About

Chi Sao (Sticky Hands) is a Wing Chun Kung Fu training exercise used to develop touch sensitivity (as well as having many other benefits). Enhancing this ability will enable you to read your opponents' intentions and respond to his movements much faster than you could by eye alone.

The aim of this publication is to enable the users to self-learn Chi Sao in a way where it is applicable to real fighting scenarios, and to do so to a standard where they can then continue to progress on their own. It does not attempt to delve into the inner workings of Wing Chun or any other fighting methods.

It is recommended to use this publication in conjunction with or as supplementary training to **How to Street Fight** by Sam Fury.

The contents are given in a specific order starting with basic positioning, progressing through numerous drills and then moving onto Free Flowing Chi Sao. Follow this order for maximum benefit.

Drills

Drills help develop proper technique and spontaneous reactions. Once this is achieved, move onto the next drill and/or Free Flowing Chi Sao.

If there is a size difference, adjust the angle of your body so energy is directed towards your opponent.

When-ever there are two people in a demonstration, the person on the left (the female) will be referred to as P1 and the person on the right (the male) will be referred to as P2. Practice all drills from both sides of the body. Use padding if needed, but gloves are cumbersome. Adjust the movements so they work for you.

Centerline Principle

(Joan Sien/Jong Sum Sin)

The centerline is an imaginary line that runs vertically down the center of the body. Attack and defense are based on this line i.e. guide incoming attacks out of your center, past your body. Attack your opponent along his center.

Always keep the centerline of you and your opponent in mind when fighting. Have control of your centerline whilst penetrating his.

Stance

In order to enable ease of transference from practice to real life, stand in the Fighters Position. The following description of the Fighters Position is taken from **How to Street Fight** by Sam Fury.

Your Lead Side

If your right leg is forward most, then your right side is your lead and your left side is your rear. When fighting, have your strong side as your lead most of the time, but train on both sides. Most of your strikes come off your lead.

Stand with your feet shoulder width apart and take a natural step back. Put a slight bend in your knees. Your body is relaxed with a slight forward lean. Find the point at which you are most balanced. Be firm and flexible as opposed to stiff and rigid. To test, have someone push you from the front.

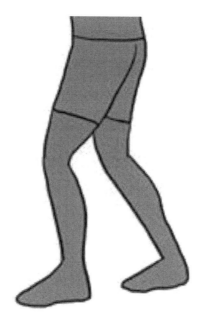

Hand Positions

There are 3 main hand positions used in Chi Sao. They are Tan Sao (Palm up Block/Taun Sao), Bong Sau (Wing Arm Block/Bon Sao) and Fook Sao (Bridge-On Arm Block/Fok Sao/Fuk Sao). Practice each of these hand positions separately as well as switching from one to the other.

Tan Sao

Tan Sao is used to limit the opponents' ability to strike straight in. Drive it forward from the center of your body in a slight upward motion.

Ensure the following;

- ⋏ Your palm is open, fairly flat and facing the sky.

- ⋏ There is approximately a 30 degree bend at the elbow.

- ⋏ The whole arm is very slightly towards your centerline.

Bong Sau

Bong Sau is used to redirect the opponents' attack to a neutral position. It is best used when you are already in contact with the opponents arm.

Ensure the following;

- ⅄ The elbow is pointed straight out and slightly in.
- ⅄ The forearm is angled at a 45 degree downward slope in towards the centerline.
- ⅄ The forearm is also angled 45 degrees forward.
- ⅄ The wrist is in the centerline.
- ⅄ The elbow is higher than the wrist.
- ⅄ The hand/fingers continue in the same direction as the forearm.
- ⅄ The upper arm is in a fairly straight line, pointing to the front.
- ⅄ The angle of the elbow is slightly greater than 90 degrees.

Fook Sao

This defensive position is placed over your opponents' arm. Exact positioning is adjusted to fit the situation and is often described as either high or low.

Ensure the following;

- ⅄ The elbow is about 6-8 inches from the body and angles in towards the center of your body.
- ⅄ The forearm angles up with the hand open and the fingers hooked down towards the wrist.

Dan Chi Sao

Single Sticky Hands/Don Chi Sao/Doan Chi

The movements in this drill are not to be applied with intent of striking. They are for teaching the feeling of movement and, to begin with, are to be performed gently.

Contrary to the name, it is the forearms that 'stick', not the hands. They stay in touch throughout the entire drill.

P1's right arm is in Tan Sao. P2 adopts Fook Sao with his left arm on top of P1's arm. P2 presses his elbow inwards towards his centerline. Both exert a slight forward pressure.

In one motion, P1 uses the Tan Sao to guide P2's left arm off the centerline then attempts to strike with the same hand. P2 defends by dropping his elbow down and inward.

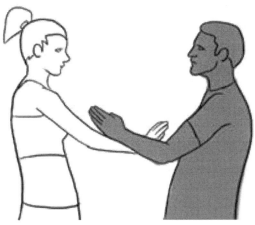

P2 attempts to strike P1's face. P1 defends with Bong Sao. P1 and P2 return to the starting position. They repeat the drill.

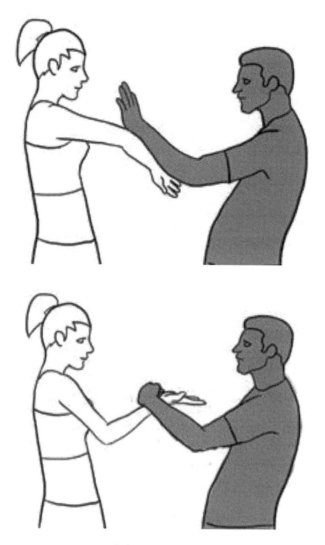

Double Dan Chi Sao

This is the same as Dan Chi Sao but with P1's free hand in a Low Fook Sao over P2's Tan Sao. This position does not change whilst the other hand performs Dan Chi Sao as normal. At the completion of one complete round, switch arms. Practice until the switch between arms is seamless.

Luk Sao

Rolling Arms/Lop Sao/Lok Sao

Luk Sao is the base of Chi Sao. Practice it on its own until fluid before incorporating attack and defense drills. Throughout the movement, keep the shoulders relaxed and apply a slight forward pressure.

Note: If your hand positions are correct, forward pressure will automatically be maintained. If your opponent removes opposing pressure, your hand will strike forward by reflex.

Luk Sao is basically moving between 2 positions. From Bong Sao and Low Fook Sao, to High Fook Sao and Tan Sao.

P1's right hand is in Tan Sao. P2's right hand is in Bong Sao. Both of their other arms are in the Fook Sao position situating over their partners opposing arms i.e. right on left, left on right. P1's Fook Sao is in a high position whilst P2's is low. Constantly press the elbow of the Fook Sao into the centerline.

P1 rotates her right elbow up, keeping the wrist in towards her centerline. As her elbow rises up to shoulder height, her forearm drops into the Bong Sao. Her left hand stays in Fook Sao throughout the movement, but moves to a low position. Keep the elbow down on the Fook Sao or forward pressure will be lost.

As P1 one does the above, P2 drops his Bong Sao back down into Tan Sao. As his Bong Sao drops, he moves his wrist outward and the elbow lowers back into its drawn-in position of the Tan Sao. As his Bong Sao settles into a Tan Sao, his Fook Sao moves from low to high while staying in contact with P1's right Bong Sao.

They then reverse the roll and return to the starting position.

All this is done in a flowing manner and it is important to do it with intent. Turn and push to interlock the hands. Be tense but flexible.

All drills from now on start from Luk Sao, unless otherwise stated.

When explaining when to initiate a drill sequence from Luk Sao, the terms 'high or low point/position' are used. This does not mean the movement is to be started at the very highest or lowest point. The exact point of where one should begin a technique is impossible to describe. With practice you will discover the best timing.

Basic Attack

P2 grabs P1's arms. His right hand grabs the inside of P1's left and his left hand grabs the outside of her right. P2 shifts his body to his left, whilst directing P1's arms forward and to the right.

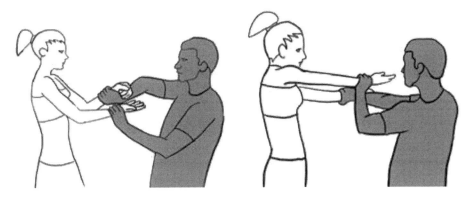

Whilst still gripping with his right arm, P2 uses his left hand to apply pressure just above the elbow, (towards the shoulder). If it is below the elbow P1 will be able to elbow P2.

P2 moves into P1 as he continues to push on P1's arm. He strikes P1's mid-section with his right hand as he moves in.

Defense against the Basic Attack

As P1 attempts the Double Arm Grab, P2 relaxes his upper body. He must keep grounded through his legs to avoid being pulled off balance.

As P1 moves in to press P2's arm, P2 turns toward her and deflects her arms away. P2's left arm angels down sharply to suppress both of P1's hands. At the same time, P2's right hand strikes P1's mid section.

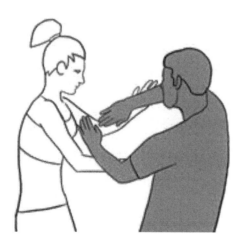 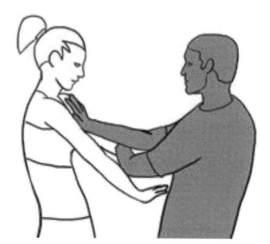

The Four Positions

There are four positions in which the arms can be in relation to the opponents guard.

1. Right Out, Left In

2. Left Out, Right in

3. Both Out

4. Both In

In the left picture they are Right Out, Left In. In the right they are Left Out, Right In.

In this picture, P1 is Both Out. P2 is Both In. In this case P1 is using a High Fook Sao and Tan Sao, and P2 is using a Tan Sao and Bong Sao.

Changing Positions

P1 is in Both Out position.

As P1's right arm gets to the low position it circles underneath P2's left hand to adopt the Left Out, Right In position. She does the same thing with the left arm to adopt the Both In position.

Right Out, Left in Attack

P1 is in the Right Out, Left In position.

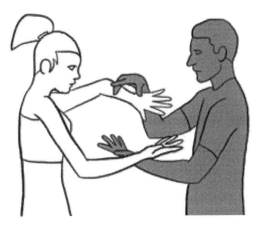

As P1's right arm gets to a high position, her left arm comes up to the outside of P2's left arm.

P1 uses both hands to grab P2's left arm above the elbow (closer to the shoulder). She pulls him in a little which exposes his ribs for attack.

If P1 pulls P2 in too much, or if P1's elbows are not jammed onto her frame when she pulls P2 in, then P2 will be able to shoulder barge her.

The following two pictures show the ideal structure of the arms to 'jam' your elbows into your frame.

Left Out, Right in Attack

P1 is in the Left Out, Right In position. As P1's right arm reaches a high point she simultaneously grabs P2's right wrist with her left hand and pushes forward with her right hand towards P2's right shoulder.

If P2 resists P1's right arm push, P1 can step in and let her right elbow collapse over P2's arm and into his centerline.

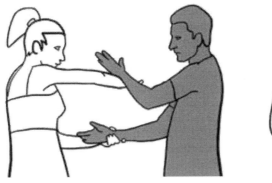

She can follow up with a strike.

Alternatively, P1 can guide his left hand to the outside with her right.

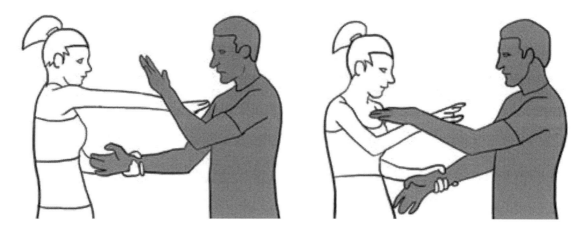

Then strike his neck or head.

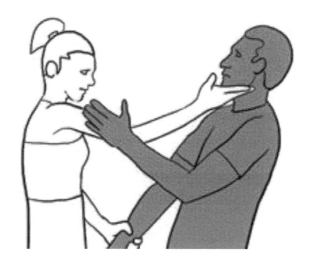

Both Out Attack

P1 is in the Both Out position.

As P1's right arm gets to a high point, she uses it to push on P2's left arm. As she does this, her left arm comes across her own body and pushes on P2's left arm just above the elbow.

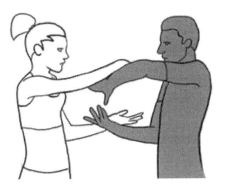 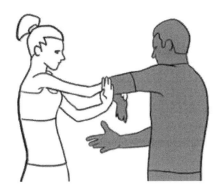

By using her right arm to suppress P2's left arm across his own body, P1 creates a situation where it would be difficult for P2 to defend against P1's strike.

P1 can either strike P2 in the head, or continue to guide P2's arm across his own body and strike his ribs. If P1 engages too low on P2's arm (closer to the wrist) he will be able to close in and elbow her.

Note: The following pictures below are shown from the opposite side as above.

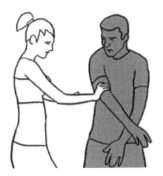 

Both In Attack

P1 is in the Both In position.

As P1's right arm comes up she circles it over both of P2's arms.

As she presses down with her right, her left comes through to strike. She can step in to close the gap if needed.

24

Pa Da

P1 is in the Left Out, Right In position. When her right arm is in a high position, she simultaneously brings her right down onto P2's right arm and brings her left hand up vertically to block P2's left arm.

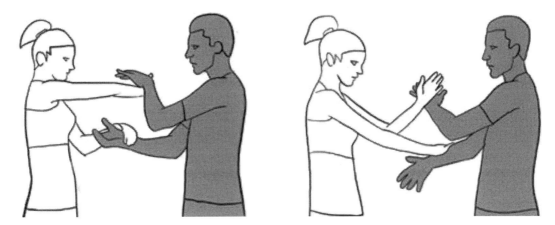

She steps through (if needed) to strike with her right.

P2 may push forward on P1's left arm before P1 has a chance to strike.

P1 can counter this by bringing her right arm to the inside of P2's left arm and moving it off the centerline whilst striking with her left.

This drill can be 'doubled up' either by switching over to the other side, or just repeating it on the same side.

Tan Da

P1 is in the Left Out, Right In potion. As her left arm comes down she switches her right hand to a palm up position (Tan Sao) to open P2's centerline.

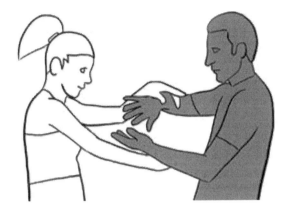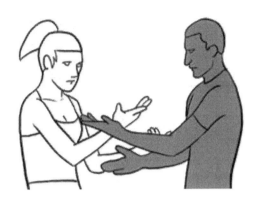

P1 strikes with her left.

As P1 strikes with her left, P2 may deflect by bringing his right hand in and up.

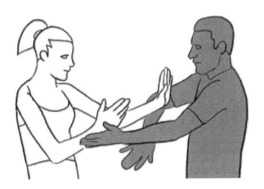

P1 can strike with her right.

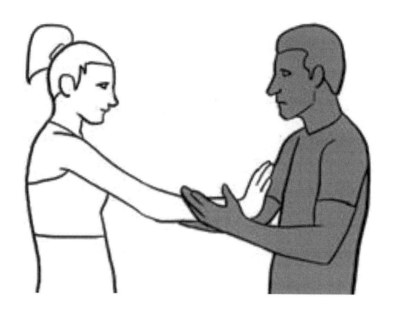

Multiple Strikes

P1 is in the Left Out, Right In position. As her right arm reaches a high point she brings it down over P2's right arm. At the same time, her left arm comes up to the outside of P2's left arm and brings it down to cross over his right.

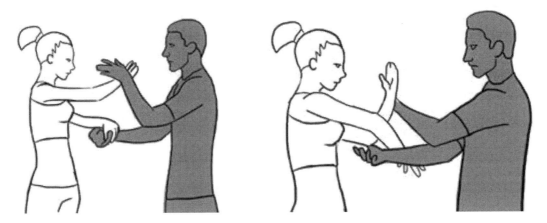

P1 pulls her left arm out and uses it to cover the top of P2's right arm.

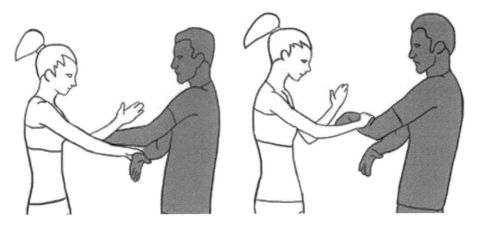

She suppresses P2's arm and strikes with her left, then her right, then again with her left.

Notice that whichever hand she is striking with, the other comes down to cover P2's hands.

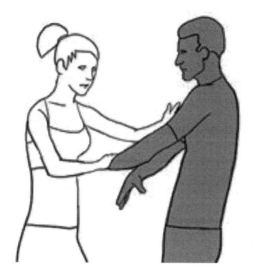

Multiple Strikes Defense

The start is the same as Multiple Strikes, but this time P1 steps in to punch. As P1 strikes, P2 steps back and deflects the strike. P1 steps forward for a second strike. Again, P2 steps back and deflects the strike. This can continue.

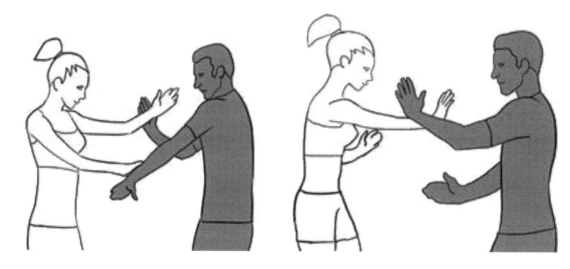

Elbow

P2 is in the Left Out, Right In position. As his right arm reaches a high point he simultaneously grabs P1's right wrist with his left hand and brings his right elbow over P1's left arm. P2's right arm continues down to grab P1's forearm. He steps forward driving his elbow into P1.

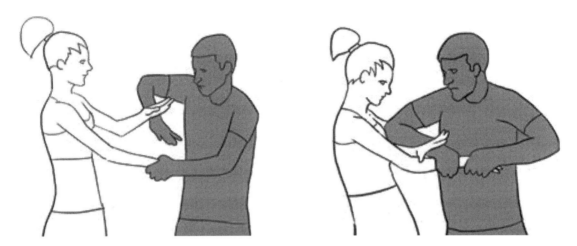

An alternative to driving in the elbow is for P2 to use his left elbow to trap P1's arm and strike her with his left.

Jud Da

P1 is in the Left Out, Right In position. As her left arm reaches a high position her right arm comes underneath and to the outside of P2's right arm.

She grabs P2's right wrist, pulling him down and forward. As P1 pulls P2 in she strike to his neck with her left. P2 raises his hand to block the incoming strike. P1 pushes down on P2's arm just above the elbow to initiate an arm break.

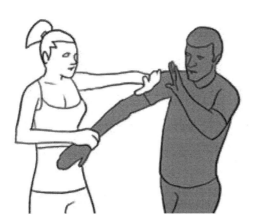 

Here is what it looks like from the other side.

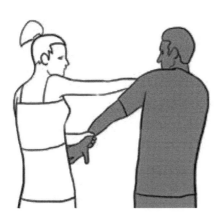 

Gum Sao

P2 is in the Left Out, Right In position.

As his right arm reaches a high point he brings his left arm across his body and to the outside of P1's left arm. He starts to push P1's right arm down with his left arm, then replaces his left with his right and continues to push her arm all the way down into the left side of her body so she cannot use it.

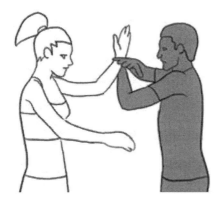 

P1 turns back towards P2. As she does this, she sweeps her right arm across her body and under P2's left arm. She then retracts her left arm and straightens her right arm towards P2.

 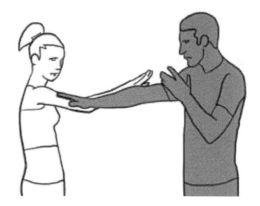

P2 uses his left hand to push down on P1's right arm. He attacks P1 with his right.

Gum Sao 2

This drill starts the same as Gum Sao but this time P1 is the initiator.

P1 is pressing on P2's right arm with her right arm. P2 uses his left arm to sweep P1's arm off his arm from the inside out.

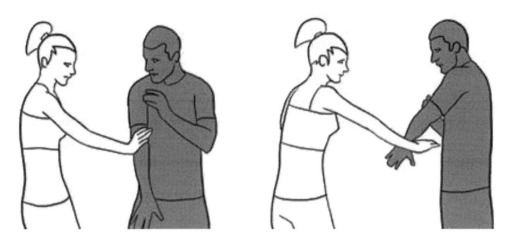

He guides P1's arm out and attacks with his right.

Neck Grab

P1 is in the Left Out, Right In position. When her left hand is at a high point her right arm comes under P2's right arm. With her right hand, P1 pushes P2's arm into his own body. She pushes just above the elbow. From here she can attack his ribs.

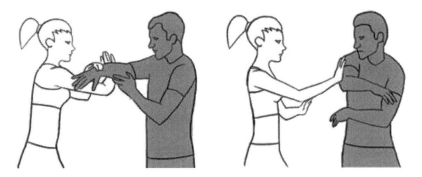

P2 may try to close in. As he closes the gap, P1 guides his elbow down. She uses P2's momentum to get him close and applies a neck grab.

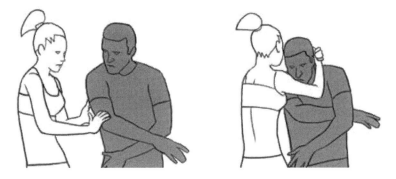

It is important for P1 to lock her leg into P2's. If she leaves a gap, P2 can knee her.

Chao Chong Kuen

P1 is in the Left Out, Right In position. When her right hand is in a high position, she uses her left hand to grab P2's left wrist. P1 pulls P2's left arm forward as she thrusts her right hand under P2's left arm and into his jaw.

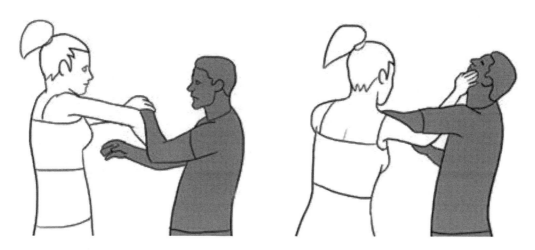

Lap Sao

Deflecting Arm Drill/Lop Sao/Larp Sao

P2's right arm is in Bong Sau and P1's left arm is in a Vertical Palm Heel with her forearm resting on P2's right forearm. Both of their other hands guard their own centerlines.

P2's left hand presses onto P1's left forearm and his right hand retracts then attacks with a Palm Heel. P1 defends the strike with Bong Sau.

From here they swap 'roles' i.e. P1's right hand presses onto P2's right forearm and her left hand strikes. They repeat this process.

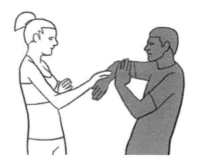

Lap Sao Attack

P1 strikes at P2 with her left. P2 defends with his right arm using Bong Sao. Both of their other hands guard their own centerlines.

P2 angles his right arm up to deflect P1's left arm out of the centerline. At the same time, he steps in and uses his left hand to press P1's right hand against P1's left bicep. P2 strikes with his right.

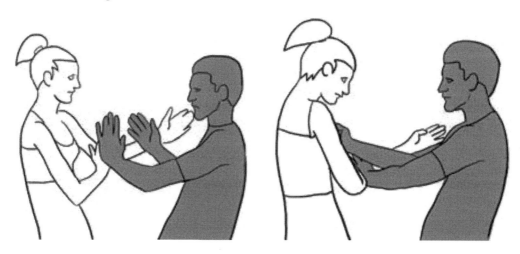

Arm Break

P1 is in the Both Out position. As her right hand gets to a high point, her left arm comes up to the outside of P2's left arm and grabs him by the wrist.

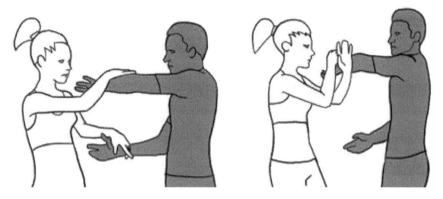

P1 pulls and twists P2's left arm to straighten it. P1 can either strike with her right or press on P2's elbow for an arm break.

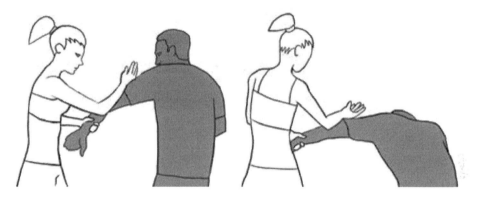

As a defense, P2 can push into P1. To prevent this, P1 can step back.

Knee

P1 is in the Both In position. When her right arm is at a high point, she brings her left arm under P2's left arm. She grabs P2's left arm with both hands, above his elbow.

 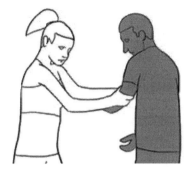

P1 pulls P2 in close and drives her knee into his thigh. She can do this with either knee. This will stun P2 and give him a 'dead leg'. She can follow up with hand strikes.

P1's knee needs to come on top of P2's knee; otherwise P2 can defend his thigh.

If P1 pulls P2 in too close then P2 can attack.

Stepping

P1 has her right side forward in a fighting stance. P2 is the same. P2's left hand grabs P1's right (forward most) hand. P1's left hand grabs P2's right hand.

P1 lunges forward with her right leg and her left leg follows. As she does this, P2 steps back with his right leg and his right leg follows.

P1 steps forward in this manner a couple of times, then P2 steps forward a couple of times. Do this back and forth.

P1 and P2 must keep grounded in a strong base or can be caught off-balance.

If either of them decides to step through to change their lead leg, the other must do the same. If not, it can result in being 'tied up'. If P2 fails to retreat as P1 steps forward, she can trip him.

If P2 kicks P1, she can defend by angling her lead leg inwards. If P2 pushes too hard, P1 can let him in and apply a head grab. If P1 pushes and P2 lets her in, she can avoid being controlled by driving her elbow into him.

Extended Drill

P1 is in the Left Out, Right In position. When her right arm is at a high point, she brings her left hand across her body and under P2's left arm. With her left hand, she grabs and directs P2's left arm across their bodies and strikes with her right.

 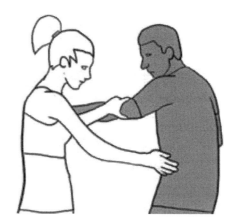

P2 strikes with his right but P1 defends with her left. P1 does this by using her right hand to grab and pull P2's left arm. At the same time, she uses her left hand stop P2's right hand at the shoulder. Alternatively, P1 could strike at P2's head.

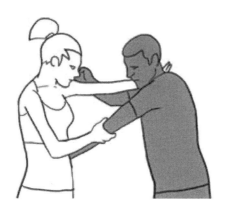 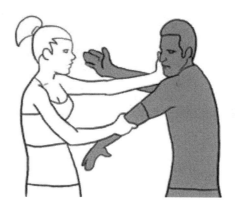

If P1 pulls P2 in too far or grabs his arm too low then P2 may close into her. If P2 tries to close in and P1 realizes, she can knee his thigh.

Extended Drill 2

P1 is in the Left Out, Right In position. When P1's arm is at a high point she brings her left arm under P2's left arm. She grabs P2's wrist and pulls him down and forward. As P2 comes in, P1 uses her right arm to strike at P2's neck.

If P2 blocks P1's strike, P1 can grab and pull his right arm.

This will expose his ribs for attack.

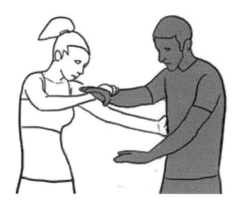

P2 can deflect P1's body strike by dropping his right elbow down to protect his ribs. If he does this, P1 can step through and drive her right elbow into his mid-section.

P2 may step back in defense. P1 can extend her arm to strike.

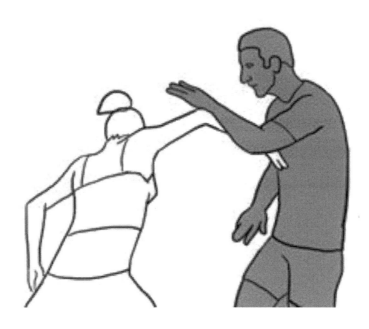

Kick

P1 is in the Left Out, Right In position. At the right time, she simultaneously grabs the wrists of P2 i.e. her right hand grabs P2's left wrist and her left hand grabs P2's right wrist.

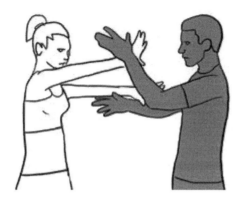

She brings them to a low position and kicks him in the thigh.

She could kick him in the stomach but there is a greater chance of being pushed off balance.

Kick 2

P1 is in the Left Out, Right In position. As P1's right hand reaches a high point, she brings her left hand across her body and under P2's left arm. She grabs P2's left wrist and kicks his leg.

If P2 is too close to kick, then P1 can grab his arm with both hands and knee him from a variety of angles.

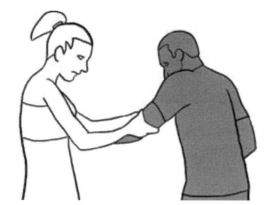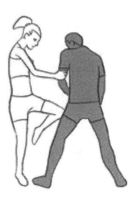

Locking her elbows to her torso will help control distance and balance.

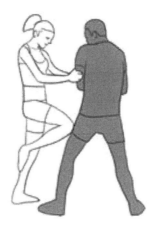

Free Form Chi Sao

Now that you have a basic understanding of various techniques, it is time to go into Free Form Chi Sao.

Although often referred to as Sticky/Sticking Hands, the goal of the exercise is not to stick to your opponent. Instead, like all fighting, the aim is to protect oneself whilst exploiting your opponents' openings.

Like all sparring, it is a good time to test what works and/or what reactions are formed from your actions. Here are some general tips;

- Don't pull your limb back in preparation for a strike.

- Be aware of force. If he uses too much, give then attack. If his force is too weak, attack through his defense.

- Strike only when there is an opening. This is especially true if kicking.

- Always be aware of distance.

- Stay on the centerline and respond to his actions. Let it flow.

"Stay with what comes, follow through as it retreats, and spring forward as our hand is freed."

- Wing Tsun Motto

Free Form Sticky Hands Variations

There are many ways to vary Chi Sao apart from just 'going at it'. The only limit is your imagination. Here are a few ideas;

- Start over whenever a strike makes solid contact. This is good when first learning.

- With or without footwork. Without footwork is good when first learning.

- One arm or two arm. Can also try cross arm e.g. right arm vs. right arm.

- Just defend or attack.

- Blindfolded. Great for advanced training in sensitivity. Start slow.

- Stop after every move. This gives you time to think/talk about your technique and your next move. Aim to streamline your movements.

Chi Gerk

Sticky Legs

This is Chi Sao for the legs. Since the legs are stronger and harder to relax, they are more likely to get fatigued. Preparing them with leg strengthening exercises will help.

Leg Preparation

P1 and P2 stand facing each other. They extend their arms in front of them and use each other for support to help balance each other during the exercise. P1 lifts her right leg off the ground, keeping her lower leg vertical. P2 raises his left leg, angles his lower leg inward and presses it onto P1's lower leg.

P1 presses her leg inwards whilst P2 presses his leg outwards. Repeat the exercise on both legs from both sides.

Chi Gerk Drill 1

P2 kicks with his left. P1 defends by cross stomping P2's lower left leg with her right.

P1 quickly switches legs and kicks to the inside of P2's left leg, then down onto his right knee.

Chi Gerk Drill 2

P1 kicks with her right leg. P2 redirects it with his lower left leg, and then kicks P1's left leg.

Chi Gerk Drill 3

P1 begins to kick with her right leg. P2 deflects it with his right lower leg. P2 then simultaneously kicks P1's right leg and strikes at her head.

Free Form Chi Gerk

Like Free Form Chi Sao, the ways to train in Chi Gerk is only limited to imagination. Many of the ideas from Chi Sao can be adapted. Here are a couple of extras;

⅄ Lock arms and try to control each other's leg(s) while kicking out the supporting one.

⅄ Just add kicks and sweeps to Chi Sao, especially if your hands are in a 'stale mate'.

Index

Thank You for Reading

HOW TO DO CHI SAO

WING CHUN STICKY HANDS

A bibliography can be found at **SurviveTravel.com/resources**

If you found the information in this book useful, please let others know by leaving a review from where you purchased this book.

If not, please voice your concerns and/or suggestions directly to the publisher at **SurviveTravel.com/contact.**

Other titles by Sam Fury can be found at

Amazon.com/author/samfury

Related Reading

How to Street Fight by Sam Fury

Follow SurviveTravel.com Authors

SurviveTravel.com

Twitter.com/Survive_Travel

Facebook.com/SurviveTravel

Made in the USA
Middletown, DE
08 January 2015